WITH WING UNSPENT

WITH WING UNSPENT

SELECTED POEMS, 1930-1995
BY CATHERINE BEEN HANSEN

G O L D E N Q U I L L P R E S S

Manchester Center, Vermont
Publishers Since 1902

Library of Congress Catalog
Card Number 95-077164

I.S.B.N. 0-8223-0502-3

Printed in the United States of America

1-800-258-1505

ALSO BY CATHERINE BEEN HANSEN:

Frugal Chariot *(written as Karen Arnold)*

C O N T E N T S

J U S T I F I C A T I O N

The fringed polygala bejewels the shade,
And to the wind tips its magenta crest.
It cannot cloak the slopes of Everest,
Or feed the multitudes in some crusade;
It does not furnish placards to persuade
The populace of wrongs to be redressed,
Nor is it tried in any cancer test,
And yet it lifts its blossom, undismayed.

My flower-lyrics bloom to no avail
Among the quill crops of utility—
History, law, and logic, centuries grown.
Yet, though creeds die, and mighty empires fail,
My theme shall be renewed perennially,
And eons hence, love's flower be freshly blown.

D E T O N A T I O N

One kiss, my sweet!
Surely decorum's not above
One kiss, my sweet?

How rapidly your pulses beat!
Learn, in our present game of love
The endless chain-reaction of
One kiss, my sweet!

TOO DEEP FOR WORDS

Love is too deep for words,
But the warbler knows the theme,
And tells in wordless melody
The glory of my dream.

Love is too deep for words,
But the torrent knows my heart,
And pours out song to speed the night
That we must be apart.

And ever as I listen
To water-sound and birds,
The whole wide world seems eloquent
Of love too deep for words.

To A Potential Puck

If I could be a flower,
And you a winged sprite,
Searching in the darkness
For refuge from the night,

I would not be a gentian,
That dusk should curl me tight,
Leaving no yielding crevice
Where stubborn lobes unite;

But I would be the primrose,
Responsive to your plight,
That you might see my golden door,
And enter, with delight.

O F F E R I N G

I dried my hair in the sunlight,
Tossing its wheat-gold mist;
For you I would keep it forever
In its summer, Midas kissed:
So fragrant, soft, and comet-bright
Its morning mist.

I shed my garments at nightfall
Before my silvered glass;
Slender and honey-hued I swayed
Like candle-flame on brass:
So take me, meshed within your trawl
As in this glass.

I N V O C A T I O N

Speak to me in the sigh of the pine tree tossing,
In the whispered, tender, accents of the sea;
In all the softened voices of night descending,
Speak to me.

Sing to me in the trill of a bird at dawning,
In the sound of the brook, which carols
    unceasingly,
In the cricket's chirp, and the hornet's busy
    humming,
Sing to me.

Fondle me with the touch of a leaf's caressing,
With a breeze's hands, where only your own
    should be,
With the stroke of rain, the encompassing arms
    of sunlight,
Fondle me.

Stay with me in the shadow which follows ever,
In the sound that echoes my footsteps from cliff
    and tree,
In the air I breathe, and the earth I tread; as
    steadfast,
Stay with me.

WINTER WELCOME

When snow across a barren landscape drifts,
The chickadee knows well my casement ledge,
And comes undoubting, to receive my gifts:
A bit of seed, an ivory suet wedge.

As confident of welcome, and a crumb
To soothe my inner need, ever at will,
Storm-buffeted, my hungering heart may come
And find its morsel on your window sill.

REPERTOIRE

How shall I dance for my love? Shall I be fey?
Dizzily pirouetting, around and around,
Swooping as swallows sweep earthward,
     then up and away,
Spurning the ground?

How shall I dance for my love? Shall I be shy?
Stepping as lightly as fawns which roam
     through the glade,
Only a moment seen, then lost to the eye
In the dappled shade?

How shall I dance for my love? Shall I be coy?
Spreading a painted fan with deliberate art,
Promising yet withholding a woman's gift of joy,
Though it break his heart?

How shall I dance for my love? Languidly,
     longingly?
Leaden of limb, too listless to raise a hand,
Moving as moth to the flame, as stream to
     the sea,
When his eyes command?

How shall I dance for my love?

R E A S S U R A N C E

I could no more turn faithlessly from you
Than from the shadows at the sun's first light,
The mossy rose-buds, misty in the dew,
The lissom leaping of a fawn in flight.
I could not be inconstant to the gold
Of buttercups that trace the brooklet's side,
Nor to your smiles of tenderness, which hold
All beauty I have known, intensified.

Only when dawn no more awakes my song,
And sunset skies no more delight my gaze;
Only when scent of lilac, sweet and strong,
Fails to evoke my lyric words of praise,
May it be said that I have grown less fond—
That your heart spoke, and mine did not respond.

DEPENDENT

I am a bow that is always taut,
Bent to your will.
Loose but your hold, and I am as naught,
Quivering, then still.

No more does joy, like the soaring dart
Spring from your hand;
The strength of linen and hickory heart
Must fail, unmanned.

Only for you I hum my song,
For you I bend.
Be gentle, archer. Mine the thong
You break, or mend.

N U P T I A L S

No wedding bells spoke to the balmy day;
No bridesmaids, two by two,
    trod down the aisle;
No rosy girls strewed flowers on the way—
No priestly blessing, no paternal smile
To cherish as our own.
We were alone.

Yet hallowed was the day I went to you,
And vows were in the gaze you turned on me.
Bells rang within our hearts, as clearly true,
And flowers strewed our path, as fair to see,
Though wildly grown.

But be it known,
While other bonds have been dissolved in tears,
Our unbound love has lasted through the years.

S T A L W A R T

Some loves are like the balsam, quick to grow;
But like the tree, too frailly linked to life,
Fall victim to the adverse winds which blow,
Or meekly yield to axe or whittling knife,
Or snap beneath a winter's weight of snow.

But ours like ironwood slowly did emerge,
Struggling from shadow to the upper light
For long, slow years; and now upon the verge
Of heaven stands secure, a stalwart sight,
Repulsing storm and blade, resisting blight.

N E E D

As the tree possesses the blossom,
The wave caresses the shore,
Possess and caress me through the night,
Close to my heart once more.

As on the far horizon
Darkness embraces the light,
Embrace me, efface from my memory
The years' relentless flight.

But as the tulips hold dewdrops,
The fruit enfolds its seed,
Hold me, enfold me tenderly,
For you are all I need.

P A R A D I S E

If evening meant your step upon the gravel
    walk outside—
Upon the stoop—upon the sill—your hand upon
    the door,
And as a gentle pressure set it slowly swinging
    wide,
The evening sunlight softly laid your shadow on
    the floor;

And if my eager greeting in that quiet corridor
Could serve the fabric of your life, from dross,
    to alchemize
Into a golden armor which would shield you
    evermore—
Could make the dawn of gladness break across
    your guarded eyes,—
Ah, sweetheart! I would never need a distant
    Paradise!

SEASONAL BOUNTY

What can I give you when I am old?
Summer is lavish with sparrow song,
Shimmer of leaf and lily-gold;
Winter is barren and bleak and long—
And cold!

Youth can be prodigal with delight:
Firm, smooth flesh for your hands to hold,
Beauty, a benison to your sight,
Sweetness, a scourge through the
    passionate night.
But what can I give you when I am old?

R E P R O A C H

You weave the warp and weft of all my days
For idle pastime, as an infant plays.

You bring me joy,
Giving a reckless lilt
To carefree days.
You bring me blame
To weight my lids with guilt
Beneath your gaze.

You bring despair,
Locking my heart out in the night,
To feel;
And then, with hope,
You welcome it into the light,
To heal.

You weave the dark and bright threads into one;
But do you stop to think what you have done?

W I S H E S

I wish I were a butterfly, on spangled wing
Soaring, sailing, drifting, fluttering,
Perching precariously upon a stalk of wheat
While you sway nearby on a snowy marguerite,
With no one to whisper, *"How very indiscreet!"*

Would you were a kinglet, swinging on a stem,
Pouring out your love in song, with winning
     stratagem;
Cocking your head, to display your ruddy crest,
Stealing sidelong glances that observe my
fluttering breast,
And no one to scathe us with,
    "How boldly unrepressed!"

Oh, to be two dragon-flies, darting over waves,
Far above the sandstone bluff, with its
     storm-cut caves;
Spreading wings of sheerest tulle against the
     sapphire blue,
Meeting in mid-heaven for a lovers' rendezvous,
And none near to prophesy, *"He'll be untrue!"*

THE WHETTED WORD

If ever this bright rapture should depart,
Leaving you cold to me, and all I meant
Of youthful fire and ecstasy is spent
Futilely, in the ashes at your heart;
Seek not by guile to mitigate the blow,
Pretending to a fondness long since fled;
Nor pile the charred sticks, where that
    spark is dead,
To kindle in your heart a feebler glow;

But as the woodsman, singling out a tree,
Measures its stature with a practiced eye,
Then calmly marks the place where it will lie;
Whet the bright axe, upraise it fearlessly,
And *(like that fated monarch of the wood)*
Bring me down proudly, as I always stood.

F O G B O U N D

The geese are flying, wheeling and crying,—
Lost in the fog tonight;
Not in the sun-bright arrow
Which marked their northward flight;
Not as their shaft flies, piercing the soft skies
Beneath a harvest moon,
But with ranks torn and journey-worn
Over the dark lagoon.

My spirit gropes for its dreams and hopes
In a fog that does not lift,
While phantom fears in robes of tears
Across my landscape drift.
Uttering its soft wail, it strives to pierce the veil
Which masks the upper skies,
Seeking the southland of your love,
The summer of your eyes.

TORN PATTERN

I saw a pattern of bright birds
Against a joyful day,
Rhythmic in flight;
Perhaps too young and fearless,
Much too blithe.
(Forgive delight!)

Across the singing silence
Burst
Stacatto sound;
Above, terrified pandemonium,
Below, pained shapes,
And blood upon the ground.

Beloved, I implore,
Is there to be no beauty evermore?

D u s t B o w l B e t r a y a l

As spring moves poleward on its yearly jaunts
It calls to feathered flocks invitingly,
Reminding them of northern nesting haunts,
And waking reslessness, with memory.

Across the southern marshes can be seen
The wild ducks gathering for their northward flight:
Proud mallards lifting heads of gleaming green,
Mergansers preening breasts of foamy white.

So once again this year they took the way
Which generations beat across the sky,
Learning too late that nature can betray
Her children at a waterhole gone dry.

Now for the feast of scavengers are trussed
Sleek wings and glossy necks, awry in death;
Their blue and white and green are dulled by dust.
And sand in gaping bills replaces breath.

Here ends the flight so joyously begun,
Where blank eyes stare, unblinking, at the sun.

A L I E N

I walk the woods in early May
When scarce a breeze is stirring;
The only sound upon the air
The grouse's sudden whirring.

But I am not at all deceived
By desolation, seeming
To cloak the forest, for I know
Its shadowy glades are teeming

With infant life and parent life,
But for the moment hiding
From this strange creature who, tiptoe,
So noisily is striding.

When I have passed, the fox's kits
Again will start their tumbling,
While spotted fawns, on new-born legs,
Behind the does go stumbling;

From under stones and rotten logs
The lizards will come crawling,
And once again from budding limbs
Veerys renew their calling.

When hare and mouse peer out to see
My clumsy form retreating,
They will steal forth, though warily,
And soon resume their eating.

But I must go my lonely way
Across the woods, adjusting
My ego to the fact that none
Dare gather round me, trusting.

Study In Grey And White

Grey gulls are strife.
As though to prove their power to prevail,
They swoop, to soar again into the gale,
Breasting the storm till they, exhausted, fail.
Grey gulls are youth.

White gulls are age.
Majestic figures shuttle ceaselessly
As shifts the wind; now rising gracefully,
Now drifting down air currents to the sea.
White gulls are peace.

VOICE OF SOLITUDE

Here is a stillness which none have broken:
Quiver of leaves, where kinglets swing;
Wavering grass where the red squirrels pass,
And the crickets chirp, and the locusts sing.
You have not come, or the wild things, startled,
Quickly had scurried or taken wing.

This is a silence too sure for gladness:
Shriek of a flecked hawk, overhead;
Hiss of a snake in the bordering brake,
Deer passing near with pixie tread.
All bear one message of desolation,
For, had you come, they would all have fled.

C H I C K A D E E

Chickadee upon the bough
Pouring out your rapturous song,
Know you not your fleeting Now
Will be Yesterday erelong?

Know you not that death awaits
Eager heart and beating wing?
Sharp eyes glaze and breath abates?
Yet you sing!

Yet you sing with pulsing throat,
"Love is sweet and life is fair!"
Hope and gladness in each note
Dancing on the frosty air.

As the cycle of the leaf
Clothes and strips the patient trees,
Life, to me, seems all too brief.
Tell me, please,

What the source of all your glee?
What your faith, that free of fear
You can squander joyously
Your last year?

To A Homeless Cat

I raise my head, sensing a watchful presence,
As I sit lonely, reading beneath the light,
To see two grape-green eyes wistfully gazing
Into the lamp's glow, out of the windy night—
Jade discs blazing.

Spellbound we hold each other's eyes a heartbeat,
Spanning the gulfs of nature and of space;
Fusing the worlds of man and the small furred
    creatures;
Halting the flow of time, for a breathless, wild
Moment of grace.

As I open the door, I hear a hurried thud,
An urgency of whispering feet, descending;
The silent echo of your presence strikes
My breast with loneliness for you, heartrending,
As off you scud.

Hounded beside the roads and through the woods,
Along the gutter trails, across the quay;
Forever gaunt with hunger, always tense
With watchfulness of danger; in a sense
You are like me.

CAPTIVE EAGLE

The captive eagle sits, hunched in his feathers,
Dejection and resignation in his eye;
Has he forgotten so soon his proud dominion?
The spacious panorama of earth and sky?

Lonely above the crags lies his lofty highway,
Abandoned the precipice, cloud-wrapped and dim;
On the inaccessible rock decays his eyrie,
But the desolate mountain-tops remember him.

WARNING TO LAGGARD GEESE

Cold blows the wind in the sere marshes,
Rigid each blade of grass, crisped by the frost.
Wild ones afloat on the rough tumbling waters,
Flee! Opportunity soon will be lost!

Gales whip the wild snowy banner of winter,
On each pool's border the ice shows its teeth;
Stark are the sedges that sheltered your nesting,
Cold lie the waters awaiting beneath.

Last week a line of your brothers flew southward,
Last night another was crossing the moon.
Autumn has died, like an out-blown candle;
Winter has come too soon, too soon!

MOURNING FOR PETS

They were allotted a life span short of mine;
I was condemned to a term ten times as long,
Often impaled on bereavement's poignant prong—
Denied death's anodyne.

But better my hours protracted in loneliness,
Rather my grief at their loss, than that they
     should roam,
Aged and lonely, in search of a long-lost home,
A dimly recalled caress.

All through the world, like jetsam thrown
     to the sea,
Wander the starving, the cold, abandoned strays,
Wander the lost, the cherished of former days,
Seeking security.

So while I mourn, forsaken, a scratch at the door,
Or eyes of desperation aglow in the dark
Fan to a flame compassion's failing spark,
And reluctant, I love once more.

B U T T E R F L Y

How strange that He who underneath his heel
Compressed the elements in rigid bands,
Then tore the hard crust roughly from the earth
And bent and broke it in His mighty hands;

How strange that He who dug the ocean's bed,
And mounded mountains great against the sky,
Should labor with painstaking tenderness
To fashion you, frail golden butterfly!

ABANDONED CAT

I roam the streets;
Oh, I am old and thin,
And very cold.
Will no one take me in?

My furry coat,
Once so luxuriant,
Now filled with burrs,
Is just an irritant.

Deafness blocks ears
Attuned to scampering
Of tasty mice.
Age handicaps my spring.

My home is found
Wherever my feet have led—
Beneath a bush,
Or in a ramshackle shed.

The wind intrudes
Into my lone retreat,
Bringing a threat
Of chilly rain or sleet.

I peer through windows
Where warm hearth fires glow,
Dimly recalling
Such comfort long ago.

With aching joints
I limp through life, footsore,
And scratch, disconsolate,
At many a bolted door.

A man darts out
To spurn me with a kick.
Dodging once more,
I wander, tired and sick.

Is his a heart
That never learned to ache?
Is his a heart
Which knows not how to break?

To The Red Fox

The suffering human shouts and swears aloud,
Or groans and tosses on a disordered bed;
But you, my woodland brother, facing death
With dignity unbowed,
Creep silently to hide
Within a thicket, where with muzzle red
You lick your bleeding side.

The human babe complains with lusty wail
Which pierces knifelike through the startled ear;
But silent hide the infant quail,
Informed of peril near,
More indistinct than shadows by the trail.

Just so the dappled deer
Shrinks in the mottled shade to escape detection,
While the lithe doe, its mother,
Starts bravely up to lure the hunter's steps
Off in a false direction.

O woodland brother,
Nature's forbearance often puts to shame
Our vaunted godlike claim.

ORPHAN FAWNS IN MARCH

We are the weak and wasted,
Outcast and battle-scarred,
Tottering along the narrow trails,
Ever, in fear, on guard.

Scarcity haunts the woodland paths—
Succulent buds cropped dry,
Dead leaves iced to the forest floor,
And the cedar boughs too high.

We flinch as the sharp hoofs strike our sides,
Routed by others' need—
No power to retaliate,
No mothers to intercede.

We lie in the melting snowdrifts,
Weary of wandering;
We die on the edge of winter,
Our blind eyes turned to spring.

F E R A L   A T T A C K

I saw a doe,
Her legs imprisoned in the crusty snow,
Struggling to go.

I saw her tail
Signal to warn of dogs upon her trail
I watched her fail.

Fleeing through the dell,
From the tormentors she could not repel,
She strained and fell.

With anguished eyes,
I saw the vicious dogs tear at her thighs.
She could not rise.

A passer-by,
I heard the echoes of their yelping cry,
And watched her die.

Hunting Season

When Indian summer doffs its war bonnet,
Gay with the spectrum colors of the trees,
Which bright leaves yet
Display, in drifts that swirl about our knees;
Life's current shifts,
As men, by trials beset,
Turn back to nature's verities,
To follow forest trails, and to forget.

But peace of mind, for me, will be deferred
Until the snow congeals along the fence
Like mounded curd.
For I detest the scarlet violence
Which holds no rest
Until its hues are blurred,
As winter blots out this intense
Season of fleeing buck and falling bird.

T H E H O R S E

We carried the conquerors of the world
With our courage, strength and speed.
Where civilization moved, you find
The hoof-print of a steed.

The armored, victorious knights of old
By our brawn were empowered
To spread the message of the bold
Where effete nations cowered.

From the Hippodrome to Ascot
We raced in equine beauty,
Putting our loyalty on the line
In many a test of duty.

We drew stagecoaches westward,
We carried the Pony Express,
Opening vast new lands to all
Across the wilderness.

Our psychic instincts often saved
The lives of those unable
To find water in deserts, or the way
Back to ranch and stable.

We have been exploited and abused,
Though we seldom attack in return.
Our sensitiveness is a trait
Which some *men* never learn.

What mankind owes to our faithfulness
Is to speak out, loud and bold,
Against the brutes who abandon us
To hunger, squalor and cold.

What mankind owes our intelligence
Can only be repaid
By letting us spend our declining years
In pastures dappled with shade.

WILD STALLION ON A HILL

High on a distant hill, like a white-cap reared
    on a wave,
Wild as untrammeled seas, brave as their
    storms are brave,
A stallion stands like a runner, poised for the
    race unrun,
Anointed along his flanks with the golden light
    of the sun;
Shod with the sparks of speed, brighter than
    forge can throw,
Haltered only by need for the mare who
    waits below.
Suddenly lancing the air with a neigh like a
    quivering spear,
He plunges down petrified combers, to disappear.

M Y J E W E L S

At dawning, bird song
From each ecstatic bill;
At gloaming, hyla-chime,
Like myriad sleighbells shrill.

In morning, dew-strands
Festooned along each vine;
In evening, sun-gold,
Deepening to claret wine.

On waking, bright shreds
Of dreams too frail to hoard;
On drowsing, foretaste
Of each joy, sleep-restored.

SAND SCULPTURE

We roamed Superior's shore, a happy land
Where hope soared with the silver spume upflung,
And there together, when our hearts were young,
We wrought our architecture on its strand.
A castle grew beneath your dextrous hand;
Tall turrets rose, a lifted drawbridge hung.
I watched but fearfully, with eyes which stung,
Sensing the sad impermanence of sand.

The shore is lonely now, the sands swept smooth
Where tides and summer storms have
    had their scope;
The wind blows on, still wildly flinging spray;
But there is nothing in this scene to soothe
The dreaming child who feared, yet dared to hope,
Then saw hope's tenuous structure swept away.

F A T E

Stamens and pistil and the burrowing bee,
Wreathed in fresh petals of resplendent hues,
Exemplify our human entity,
Designed to meet and fuse.

Wind, the match-maker in its ancient role
Scatters the cells on a receptive core,
As you engulfed my yearning heart and soul
With love's seductive spore.

But as the petals fade, and arid blight
Sears the green plant, and foils creation's plan,
So do the Fates, indifferently, unite
To thwart the will of man.

Or random gusts may frustrate life's design,
Directing dreams to unreceptive stone;
Then all the hopes of joy that once were mine
Perforce are overthrown.

Spring Plaint

Though many sing the paean of new birth
After the winter's dearth; though many sing
Their praise of infant spring;

Though many, schooled to silence through
    long night,
Look upward to the light, the first bright day,
Remembering how to pray;

My song is silenced. What shall it avail
That blossoms, fragile, pale, around me blow,
The day that you must go?

B A R R E N

Somewhere a picture that never was painted,
A dance which forever is shadowed in night,
Wait for the hands and the minds of our children
To bring them to light.

Denied fulfillment, with all bereaved mothers
I share inconsolable grief for their young,
Mourning a poem which cannot be written,
A carol unsung.

Weeping a drama bereft of its hero,
A statue forever encased in the stone;
Ever lamenting an orator silent,
A statesman unknown.

D A W N

We have a daughter. Behold where she dallies,
Touched by the flush of a day just begun;
Dimples like shadows asleep in the valleys,
Laughter like brooklets that leap in the valleys
Where she wades laughing awhile as she dallies,
Waiting the rising sun.

Swift as the daybreak, she comes without warning,
Tossing bright tresses like sunbeams, dawn-spun;
Lightly her feet dance to meet us each morning,
Gaily her eyes dance, reflecting the morning;
Dancing to meet us, she comes without warning
Out of oblivion.

Cherish our daughter *(her touch like the breeze's!)*
Cherish our daughter *(her smile like the sun!)*
Fleet as a fawn, she will roam as she pleases;
Never a dawn but she roams as she pleases,
Fleet as a fawn and as light as the breezes—
Changeless, till time is done.

46

WINDOW IMAGE

Hearts, like the purple finches, see deceptive
Vistas reflected, which they take as real;
And like the birds, lured to the mirrored branches,
Shatter their wings on dangers they conceal.

And you, my wayward one, my own bright
    fledgling,
Who would not heed the words, *"Thou shalt
    not pass,"*
Flew recklessly into a false illusion,
And broke your heart on its unyielding glass.

PERVERSITY

They tell me John is steady,
Considerate and wise.
(Why do I dream of an outlaw
With the devil in his eyes?)

They say that Henry wants a home
Immaculately neat.
(Why do I long for a gypsy,
Dancing on merry feet?)

They tell me Mark appreciates
The things that women cook.
(Why do I follow a wanderer
Who gives me scarce a look?)

They're sure that Percival would be
Faithful his whole life through;
(But oh, my fickle love, I still
Would take the tears—and you!)

R E A L I Z A T I O N

Starlight never whispers to me, *"Stay,"*
Now that you from out the starlit night have
gone away.

Dews can never cool this burning,
Fragrant grasses soothe this yearning,
Breezes breathe no hopeful word to foster faith
in your returning.

Spruces sigh, *"Prepare your heart for this:*
Nevermore within our shade may you receive
his kiss."

L O S T

Homesick for you,
Beneath trees where I swung in childhood;
Homesick for you,
On the shores where I once dug sand;
Seeking your face midst a thousand familiar
    strangers,
Yearning for you, in a suddenly alien land.

Wandering lost,
Over paths worn deep by my footsteps;
Wandering lost,
Across fields where I first found dreams;
Seeking the path we once trod through the land
    of gladness,
Searching for you, and the home that your
    presence seems.

RETURN TO HAPPINESS

Return to happiness, out of the maze
Of customs, laws, and crowd-dictated ways,
Where bleak frustration settles like a blight
Upon our love. Once more hope's acolyte
Return, before our verdant dream decays.

The warbler woos love in his roundelays,
The filly courts love with her eager neighs;
And I, with need more faceted, invite,
"Return to happiness!"

Back where the breeze-enchanted birch tree sways,
Back where spring flowers spill their sweet sachets,
Where every plum tree is a froth of white,
But whiter still, within the soft starlight,
The shape of her you love. One of these days,
Return to happiness.

W A K E F U L

A sound in the endless night!
Is it my love so fair?
Or the hope that nestles like a prayer
In my heart, stirring for flight?

Ah, but it strikes with a might
More than the heart can bear—
A sound in the endless night.
Is it my love so fair?

Only a breath, as slight
As a whisper on the stair;
There can be no one there.
Hope, fold your wings, despite
A sound in the endless night.

Q U E S T

I hear strange steps approach through street
    and lane,
But not the step of one awaited guest;
I hear the mirth of multitudes in jest,
But listen for one merry laugh in vain.
So, through the clutter of a lifetime's gain,
I wander as an outcast, dispossessed,
And while I go upon my endless quest
The slow moons of my summer wax and wane.

Perhaps on some far evening I shall go,
Out of life's havoc gales and battle din,
To where a crowd has sheltered, warm and gay;
And seeking idly for a face I know,
See that of all most cherished, and step in
As one returned to Eden.
    Perhaps I may.

PHANTOM GUEST

I am bound in a shroud of firelight,
Wrapped round with its cloying glow,
While you ride free on the frozen lea,
Through the gustily drifting snow.

You come with the night wind's coming;
Stray snowflakes star your hair
When I scrape a place in the frost's bright lace
To see you laughing there.

Laughing the wild wind's laughter,
Calling the wild wind's call,
You pass, and a pattern upon the glass
Where the firelight flickers, is all.

C O M M U N I O N

Across the shadowed wilderness of night
The legions of my thoughts creep silently;
They skirt the valleys, slip from tree to tree,
And like marauders, shun the dim starlight,
Lest any hostile force, taking affright,
Deny my message's delivery.

As in the past the wily Cherokee
Sped through the forest, glancing left and right
Where, in the dimness, his accustomed sight
Noted each altered form; so, secretly,
While starlight spreads its dainty filigree,
Or moonbeams dapple all the earth with white,
They strain to reach you, but are put to flight
When tuneful dawn, to truth, awakens me.

ENDURING LOVE

Silence has crept between us like a forest
Insidiously rising from the clay—
Entwining shrine and hearth in vernal meshes,
Effacing beauty in a slow decay.

The altar falls, its votaries long absent,
The fire grows cold, its keepers strayed away;
The timid deer, emerging from the shadows,
Fears not the sound of humankind at play.

Some lingering traveller, stirring in the ashes
To find a vessel green with verdigris,
Might muse upon the transience of passion,
And sigh for us, who loved so fleetingly.

O blind wayfarer! Would we leave our Eden
Without a coal to keep forever bright
The flame of rapture? Who would turn from Heaven
Once having stood in its eternal light?

Know, though bereft by all life's forfeitures
The solace of a cherished love endures.

L O S S

Who, loving bloom of bud and leafy spray,
Can yet deny
The beauty of the barren, wind-stripped tree
Sketched on the winter sky?
Or, convert of the sea,
Praise the proud sailing craft, so sleekly wrought,
Yet give the stranded hull no tender thought
As it rusts uselessly?
Who would gainsay
The loveliness of hair turned misty grey,
Its golden coin all spent to pay love's fee?

Though I would have life gay,
I learned from you
Loss has a sad, distorted beauty, too.

FINAL WISDOM

I strive to seize the wind—
To make it somehow mine;
To lull its voice and clip its wings
And wrap its legs in twine.

I try to freeze a poppy
Into an icy mold;
Its dance dismayed, its scent dispersed,
Its petals wilt and fold.

I dare to hold a sparrow
And bid him carol still;
He hunches like a stubborn child
Resistant to my will.

I long to still the tides
Upon a tranquil shore;
But still they ebb and still they flow
As surely as before.

Love is flower and bird song,
Wind, and broad, bright sea;
Trapped, it droops, or starts a frenzied
Struggle. Leave it free.

S E N S I T I V I T Y

Since love has given his caress
I am a mobile thing,
Stirred by each wind that passes,
As grasses, in the spring;

Lashed by the whip of every gale
That sweeps into the lair
Of new-born foxes, with the breath
Of death upon the air;

And like spring's promise underfoot,
Crushed by the careless tread
That, bruising countless lifting blades,
Invades the flower-bed.

The shafts of light at evening
Are each a pointed dart
Tipped with the chill of coming frost
And tossed against my heart.

I am aware of every scar—
Akin to every pain—
Since Love awoke me for his theft,
And left me in disdain.

The Master's Touch

As a harp, strung with warp of latent song,
Stirs sentient, by a loving master stroked,
And pours out melody, from molten joy
And liquid essence of past pain evoked,
My soul responds to you,
In strains of joy.

But one indifferent to its patina
Of mellow bloom, its subtlety profound,
Will snarl his fingers in the quivering strings,
Waking a dissonance of outraged sound.
Discordant, too, my song,
From ravaged strings.

HIDDEN TREASURE

When your eyes behold my face
Will your spirit seek my soul?
You will search an arid place
When your eyes behold my face.
But beneath lie beauty, grace—
Traits a poet could extol.
When your eyes behold my face
Will your spirit seek my soul?

R E J E C T I O N

Seared by first love, scar tissues now remain
To ache and shrink at the approach of heat
Near to my heart; and therefore I repeat
My prayer that you, in pity, will refrain
From rearousing consciousness of pain.
Plead not the petition of the incomplete;
Tempt not my heart with passion's bitter-sweet
Reward, for all your entreaties are in vain.

Better the anesthetic chill of ice,
Dulling my senses till they feel no more,
Though rapture must depart along with grief;
Than that a casual play of love suffice
To plant the seed of longing as before,
At risk of blight before the grain's in sheaf.

E X P E R I M E N T

Into the passive liquid of my soul,
Whose placid depths reflect no cherished face,
Drop but one tear of understanding love
To see a chemic miracle take place,
In rosy radiance of hope reborn;
While on its brink, once stagnant and forlorn,
The widening circles of fresh rapture break,
As from a stone, thrown on a tideless lake.

L I F E   S p a n

Here, in the weeping wound of a fallen tree
Whose leaves still quiver from its prolonged ordeal,
Bathed in its tears of sap lie the slow-turned years,
Round as clay vessels, smoothed on a potter's
    wheel.

Wrapped in its heart lies my fleeting childhood's
    span–
Years seeming brief in their rapid and careless
    course–
Like a girl's bracelet, golden and miniature,
Nestling enshrined here, close to my life-spring's
    source.

Childhood encompassing, widen the rings of girlhood,
Season of dreaming, dawning of bright-eyed hope,
Wherein the gold bands glow with symbolic meaning,
Guiding—not limiting—imagination's scope.

Next *(as the still pond, touched by the swan at sunset,*
Heaves where he drops, weary and overheated)
Widen the circles of rapture you stirred at my breast:
Here lies the cycle of womanhood, completed.

Once, like a satin band, lay love's chain, fitted
By you; but corroding time, which took you from me,
Made its links harsh as the rough bark,
    circumscribing
The weeping wound of this newly fallen tree.

64

COMMAND PERFORMANCE

Dance for me, waves, in your Degas flounces;
My feet are weighted, as though with lead;
Dance, dance, pose and advance.
(My heart is heavy, for hope is dead.)

Sing for me, sparrows, your throats nigh bursting—
Flowing with song—for my lips are mute;
Sing, sing; rejoice in the spring
Whose sunny promise my tears refute.

Laugh for me, brooklet; with wordless banter
Woo my heart back to a mood long lost.
Chortle with glee on your way to the sea,
Breaking the bondage of grief and frost.

Sad is my spirit, and slain by truth
My dancing and singing and laughing youth.

A T   N I G H T   I   C R Y

At night I cry,
For youth, whose early promise to excel
The years belie;
For dreams of lifelong creativity
Which go awry;
For all who fail in life, regardless of
How hard they try,
At night I cry.

At night I cry
For mothers of lost sons, whose pleas for words
Win no reply;
For refugees from war-torn lands, whose woes
Intensify;
For deaf who know no song, and blind, no sky,
At night I cry.

At night I cry
For suffering innocents who, gasping, take
Too long to die;
The ugly and deformed, cherishing hopes
Life must deny;
For all who feel disaster's cruel lash,
But know not why,
At night I cry.

At night I cry
For animals which stray far from their homes
When streams run dry;
For birds which struggle through wild hurricanes
That strike on high;
And for the joy and lavishness of love
Which passed me by,
Though calm in daylight *(I would scorn to lie)*
At night I cry.

POTENTIAL

Like a fresh bud that burgeons
When touched by the sun,
I opened my eyes
To a life just begun.

What was my promise?
What would I be?
What would my genes
And my culture decree?

Emerging a moth
With a shimmering wing,
Or rather a wasp
With its venemous sting?

An incipient artist
With flowers and shells,
Or a witch in the making—
A weaver of spells?

Perhaps a wind-dancer,
Like Hermes, wing-shod.
*(More likely a turtle
Predestined to plod!)*

A nightingale singing
From realms out of sight?
Or a mole, creeping low
In its tunnel of night?

An eager crusader
By passions consumed?
No, lacking in fervor
A dawdler, foredoomed!

THE RIGHT TO HAPPINESS

True, many people pass through life, secure
In the firm knowledge of their right to joy,
Viewing the world but as a larger toy
Bestowed to make their childhood games endure.
By nature confident, in practice sure,
They clutch at rapture till its pleasures cloy,
And, like a flower grasped too long, destroy
Its freshness, and its fragile form obscure.

But happiness, to me, has never seemed
Either my due to ask, or right to hold.
Sufficient that it comes as something dreamed,
But lost at dawn, before its bliss is told:
Frail as a violet's stem, brief as a sigh,
Rare as a rainbow, braceleting the sky.

V I S T A S

Hold to the forlorn hope, the distant dream—
The far mirage of waters, cool and deep,
Bright with a promise
Fulfillment cannot keep.

Treasure the love renounced, the rapture flown,
Fair as eternal stars, each night displayed
In constant glory;
For beauty held must fade.

Cherish the joy unwon, the goal ungained,
Like to the purple mountains far away,
Changeless forever.
Only the near decay.

INCONSOLABLE

Spring will return in downy ferns, close-curled
As notes, recording April's muted theme;
In crinkled, coral maple leaves, unfurled
Beside the cherry's foamy white racime.
The perfume of arbutus bells will blow
Over the spongy moss and musty logs;
Bloodroot will vie with bits of laggard snow,
And peeper chime will ring across the bogs.

But I am she who nurses an old wound,
Still unappeased by beauty's new display;
Knowing the caterpillar dies cocooned
That sequined wings may flutter for a day;
The bird tomorrow lifts to soar and sing
Displaces one now slowly stiffening.

THE VANQUISHED

The spirit, a linnet, caught in the lime of the
    trapper,
Stayed in its flight to the northward, following
    spring,
Lifts its bright wings in a futile gesture of soaring,
Tuned to the rapture of earth in its blossoming;
Wild with remembrance of broad fields, glowing
    at sunset,
Stirred by the longing for cool leaves, shadowing
    its nest,
Beats its fair wings, till the glutinous lure on
    the bushes
Grasps with cruel fingers that vibrant, terrified
    breast.

The spirit, a salmon, pierced by the spear of
    the fisher,
Shaken in life's final gaspings and shudderings,
Curves yet again for the leap up the foaming
    torrent,
Stirred by the thunderous music the cataract
    sings;
Arches again with a last fierce passion for
    freedom,
Haunted by dreams of still coves where the
    morning mists rise,
Until oblivion falls, and the struggle ceases:
The spirit, fettered to drudgery, finally dies.

Source Of Beauty

The tree which would conceal the flicker's nest
Must rot within its core to prove its worth;
The leaf-mould of dead loveliness must rest
Against the roots of beauty, brought to birth;
The parent snail may slowly putrefy
To feed its young; and on the ocean's floor
The heaped-up skeletons of coral lie,
That land may greet the sailor, far from shore;
And so the poet weaves immortal song
From sweetness lost, and sorrow overlong.

P E G A S U S

Bright as a snowy gull you mounted the hills of
    morning,
Scornful of sowings, disdainful of harvestings;
Spurning the shafts, flouting both bit and halter,
You soared to god-like heights in my youthful
    worshippings.

Over the rainbow bridge galloped your hoofs like
    thunder;
Golden you gleamed, where the beacon of evening
    swings;
Rhythm and power flowed through you, in deep
    Wagnerian measure;
Why, in a dull grey world, do I remember such
    things?

You were the longing of youth, its yearning lift of the
    spirit,
Bearer of inspiration, steed of imaginings;
You were the hunger, the thirst of aspiring childhood
Still innocent of defeat. Who clipped your wings?

You did not fall like a meteor, flaming in glory,
Nor like the lightning stagger, to ominous rumblings;
Only a dimness grew, to show you were gone from
    the heavens—
Gone with the soul that dreams, with the heart that
    sings.

W A S T E

Anemones that star the woods,
To die, unknown;
Seeds shaken from a poppy's pod
To fall on stone;

Initial talent overwhelmed by need,
For want of bread;
Maternal love, whose waiting cradle stands,
Untenanted;

Creations of antiquity,
Levelled by war;
Unwritten music, dying with
The troubadour;

Crops flattened by wild hurricanes,
Erasing yield;
Dead lads borne sadly by their comrades, from
The battlefield;

Burden the heart. None of life's triumphs nullify
Its random waste:
Compassion curbed by caste, genius unrecognized,
Beauty defaced.

C A G E D

The eagle tamed to a perch,
The wolf to a pen,
Learn the slow desperation
That falls on the spirit, when
The far-seeing eyes are shuttered
By the fences and walls of men:
Never to scan remote wilds
In triumph again.

He who was born to freedom
Of rebel strain
Never can wear life's fetters
But with disdain.
Doctored and fed and sheltered,
He yet knows pain—
A tiger tamed to the cage,
A bear to the chain.

N   U   C   L   E   U   S

As mists of vapor coalesce 'round motes of dust,
  to form
Each drop of rain,
And perfect pearls enfold at core, unknown,
A sandy grain;

So suffering humanity inspires creative thought,
For much great art
Secretly wraps a nucleus of pain
Within its heart.

M O D E L

Where many fell, this tree somehow survived,
Wresting from grudging earth its sinewed form;
Tough as the vitals of this rock-ribbed coast—
Sculptured by storm.

So may I, when my late December comes,
Showing my inner structure, winter-thinned,
Incline my branches like the tree, and look
Not to the wind.

DOUBTFUL CHOICE

I prized serenity: the quiet sigh
Of summer winds, the distant lazuli
Of hills down which eternal waters pour,
Low-whispering ripples on a tranquil shore,
High-flaring color in an evening sky.

While others sought the stars, to satisfy
My narrow needs, I was a stander-by;
Nothing could tempt me to the contest, for
I prized serenity.

Yet when troops quicken to the battle-cry,
And charge the foe's redoubts with banners high;
When echoes of life's mighty struggles roar,
Beating with wild insistence at my door;
Safe in retreat, I often question why
I prized serenity.

F L I G H T

The swift, sure arrow of a shrike's assault
With genus appetite;
A sudden thunder, as a partridge bursts
From cover, in shocked fright;
The upward rush of raptors, on attack
Climbing, till out of sight;
A headlong plunge of woodcock, glimpsed at dusk,
Courting, some springtime night.

The bouncing course of eager chickadees
That my feeders invite;
A blur of wings, which carry hummingbirds,
Each like a tiny sprite;
The spiral down-drift of relaxing gulls,
Gliding from airy height—
All fueled the dreams of mankind, long earthbound,
Who dared aspire to flight.

P A R A L L E L

Living restrains man, cumulatively;
He, like a steed, once wild and free,
Learns to conform:
First to the halter,
When curbed by discipline his steps first falter
From carefree speed;
Next to the bit—
Job or profession is our word for it;
Next to the harness is his spirit bent;
A summertime romance, a soft assent,
Lead to responsibility,
A heavy load;
Collared, he plods *(in blinders)* down life's road.

F O R E V E R

United in a wedding bond of concord,
Enriched with comforts years of wealth bestow,
Praised for accomplishments in art or science,
"Forever" is the fairest word we know.

Bereaved of those we held most dear when younger,
Maimed hopelessly, or suffering chronic woe,
Imprisoned with no hope of future pardon,
"Forever" is the saddest word we know.

T H E   D A N C E

The gossamer threads of cadence rule the dance.
Like puppets on fine strings, we pause, advance,
Twirl, bow, touch or embrace.
Melody lifts our mood to the sublime;
Tempo instructs our feet to tread in time—
Controls our eager pace.

We move, enchanted by the pulse of song—
Mesmerized by its beat. Oh, to prolong
Forever, its allure!
The lilting rhythm holds us in its spell;
Its throb inspires response. Harmonies swell
In strains complex but sure.

Round, square and folk dance have their devotees;
Hula and highland fling exhibits please
A homespun clientele.
Conga and samba boast a rebel's lure,
Waltz, fox trot, two-step challenge the mature,
Contending to excel.

Cake walk, cotillion, lure the social type,
Polka, mazurka, those of rugged stripe;
Ballet thrills the esthete.
The stately polonaise and minuet
Are shunned by those who clog or rumba, yet
All feel complete.

So join us in the dance! Invade the halls;
Whether a line dance or a schottische calls,
Step to its tempting measure.
The strains of sweetness or the stress of swing
Alike, lure us to shed all care, and bring
Us endless hours of pleasure.

I N S P I R A T I O N

Pegasus, steed of splendor,
Leaping the tall cloud-hurdles;
Pegasus, swiftest stallion,
Pounding the turf on high;
Loud with the sound of thunder
Rumble your hoofs, releasing
Torrents of dream, like showers
Upon an earth grown dry.

Pastured upon the welkin,
How like a god's your banquet—
Flower of rainbow border,
Grain of the golden sky.
Catching the gleam of sunset
After the earth is darkened,
You are the soul aspiring—
Spirit that cannot die.

H E R I T A G E

Out of the centuries of sacrifice,
Dreams, profound thought—
The aspirations of humanity—
A chain was wrought.

Each generation added one link, forged
In crucible of pain—
The shaping of ideals, which every age
Must struggle to maintain.

Armies have furnished millions to the cause,
Martyrs, lone sacrifice;
Through death and rack, wounds and captivity,
They paid a costly price.

Succeeding times must strengthen every bond
With welds of certainty,
Lest unenlightened hordes lose their birthright
Through idle apathy.

Or privileged parasites, with their demands
For selfish gain,
Will put such stress upon its fragile links
They break the chain.

R E F U G E E

I run in anguish with the fleeing crowd,
The sounds of battle loud
Across the land.
Following an ancient track, our frantic band
Push on, as enemy attacks intensify.
Bombs plummet from the sky,
Our walls crash down.
Once limpid streams are churned to muddy brown.

Stacatto shots assault our ravaged ears.
There is no time for tears,
No time for treasured toys,
No time to plan;
But to a man,
Spurred by the noise
We flee, abandoning all we own,
Wild to escape, no destination known.

Our courage fails
As aircraft strafe our columns on the trails.
Stampeding hordes, spearheaded by the strong,
Pushing and jostling, carry us along.
The weak give way.
There can be no delay
To succor those who falter, as the old
Struggle against the cold,
And infants wail
Or whimper their distress to no avail.

Our fallen friends are rudely rolled aside.
The hungry tide
Press on, indifferent to their pleading cries,
The mute reproach of staring, sightless eyes,
For terror drives us on.
All hope is gone.

OUR APPREHENSIVE WORLD

The world knows insecurity of late,
As hostile nations sow the seeds of fear,
Inciting restless multitudes to hate,
And forging deadlier weapons, year by year.
The traits of children yet unlonged for, lie
Within the shadow of a mushroom cloud,
For strange mutations threaten to defy
The trend to which the centuries have bowed.

Still we must hope, and dance on terror's brink,
And laugh at clowns, and whistle in the dark;
Still we must love, and weld the human link,
Endowing others with a vital spark;
Though lightning scars the dark clouds drawing near,
And thunder speaks its warning, deep and clear.

ABANDONED FARM

With what high hopes the homesteader arrived
Upon this quarter-section, long ago;
Felled the tall trees, routed the weeds which thrived,
And turned up hard-won furrows, row by row.
How patiently he set out orchard stock
Where now the stunted fruit, untended, fall;
How stoutly built his barn, and through the rock
Sunk the deep well which would outlast them all.

Where are the sons which, with his hopes, were sown?
The cities lured them with their easy gains.
Now, like a nest from which the birds have flown,
The empty farmhouse stands. No life remains.
No mower reaps the fields with busy sound,
But poplars repossess the fallow ground.

SHOPPING MALL

The farm is gone.

I took the highway back, the other day,
Seeking, nostalgically, remembered joys
When as a child I roamed a vanished way—
Bucolic years the stride of time destroys.

I sought the hedges, bright with butterflies,
The broad expanse of undulating grain,
Sleek grazing herds; only to realize
I lived within a dream, for none remain.

A blacktop armor has its gauntlet clenched
Upon the throat of what was once a stream;
Beyond its verge, the orchard trees were wrenched
Out of the earth, to beauty's silent scream.

The wrecking ball destroyed the attics where
We raided trunks for costumes as we played;
The cellar's store, in bin and earthenware,
Succumbed to the bulldozer's ruthless blade.

The occupants of barn and coop and pen
Were auctioned to their slaughter-certain doom;
Antiques from parlor, dining room and den
Went cheaply, whether worthless or heirloom.

Now gaudy, flashing neon lights entice
Where once the teeming acres gently rolled;
Forsythia and lilac paid the price
For merchandise unknown to those of old.

Rich loam succumbs as progress pushes on;
The smothered spores and seeds are buried deep;
The horses and the tractors both are gone.
While avid shopper swarm, the aged weep.

The farm is gone.

FRONTIERSMAN

He fell, unknown, who from the mountain's crest
Once saw the vistas of new lands, unsown,
And from the summit claimed the unpossessed;
He fell, unknown.

His was the lofty, though unsculptured, throne,
The noble though unrecompensing quest.
'Twas he who laid the future's cornerstone.

To his keen eyes cities made manifest,
And in his ears the airplane's coming drone.
In coonskin cap and greasy buckskins dressed
He fell, unknown.

DREAMER AT WORK

I cannot finish dusting;
No sooner do I start
Than all the motes go dancing
Their way into my heart.

I fail to pick up papers,
But step between them, while
Gleaning the bits of sunshine
That shimmer on the tile.

And when the piled-up dishes
Force my reluctant hand,
The rainbow bubbles twinkle,
And lost in dreams I stand.

L O S T   H E R I T A G E

"Grandfather, what were they?" I questioned him,
Of passenger pigeons, all their hosts now dead.
When he was young they made the sunlight dim
In passing overhead.

The trumpeter swan is slowly vanishing;
Extinction threatens, too, the whooping crane.
It well may be that there will come a spring
We look for them in vain.

Then let us bend our efforts to the task,
And save our heritage, while yet we may;
That future generations need not ask,
"Grandfather, what were they?"

C O M P U L S I O N

*(Compulsion: A neurosis characterized
by a persistent motor activity over which
the patient has little or no control.)*

You lie in a ward, unwanted,
Held by restraining bands,
Bereft of friends and family,
Kissing your wrinkled hands.

What memories lull your lonely years
Of a mother, holding her boy
And kissing his tender, untried hands
In an overflow of joy?

What recollections redeem the nights
Divested of all you cherished,
Of a bride who kissed your caressing hands
Long before your bright dreams perished?

Old one, with your saddened, sunken eyes,
Know someone understands,
As you lie in your dreary hospital bed,
Gently kissing your hands.

MEMORIAL TO PATRICIA

*(Patricia was deaf as the result of an illness
at the age of two. She was seven when she died.
Burned while her parents were absent.)*

I see her yet—
The elfin grace,
The dainty, pointed face
Lit by dark eyes
More fit for paradise;
Each dark ringlet;
The sudden, sweet, half-wild
Responsive way she smiled.
Who could forget?

All fanned the flame
Who, deaf to lonely cries,
And blind to pleading eyes,
Create a world unfit
For children born to it—
Heirs to our shame.
God mused, *"This lovely child
On earth would be defiled;"*
Then spoke her name.

A B O R T I O N

Life is unjust?
Kill, if you must
This tender human bud you hold in trust.

You've lost your man?
Slay, if you can
All linkage to survival of your clan.

You're overwrought,
So slaughter, if you ought
A latent source of talent, and of thought.

A job to fill?
Annihilate, if you will,
This font of creativity and skill.

Children are such a care,
So crush out, if you dare
Your toddler of the shining eyes and hair.

It wasn't planned,
So take a stand!
Blot out this miracle—death on demand!

C H A M P I O N

For years the old man toiled his way to town
To fill his needs, attended faithfully
By a small cur, all dirty white and brown
A mongrel of haphazard pedigree.

Then finally, as with all wanderers,
Death met him on the road, one scorching day.
A passing tourist called the officers
Who came and took the frail old corpse away.

Now his dog haunts his hovel constantly,
Awaiting his return. Through snows and suns
It lingers there, immune to bribery—
One with the noble breeds of champions.

V I O L I N I S T

My father bore more than his share of grief:
Rejected by his early family,
His body maimed, his youthful hopes denied,
He spent his years in deepest poverty.

Yet through a thing of wood and gut and steel
He somehow kept his heart forever young,
And every evening reaffirmed life's joy
With prancing bow, and dancing notes upflung.

C O M P L A C E N C Y

A Jew once hung, high on a cross
On Calvary;
While we, the people, spoke
In apathy,
"What is one life, of all who face
Catastrophe?

"We have our families, our homes,
Security.
This is a king's decree.
If we should be
Heard to protest, we could expect
No clemency."

And so we turned away our eyes
From agony;
Yet from across the sea,
On you, on me,
That shadow falls, with every new
Atrocity.

COMPASSION

Last year I read, with horror
Of how
In pity, a man shot his brother.
Last week, with a kiss of love,
I gave
An overdose to my mother.

PRELUDE TO PEACE

I love the dim cathedral hush of forests,
Where mighty boles of hemlock, oak, and pine,
Tower like ancient columns reaching skyward,
Their limbs entwined in intricate design.

Vestal as votive candles on the altar
Stand Indian-pipes arrayed, waxen and pale,
Lit by the lightning-taper of the tempest
Whose ancient ritual will soon prevail.

Thunder speaks suddenly into the silence,
And to the shadowy nave its prelude brings;
And like a choir boy, rapt with adoration,
A single wood-thrush lifts its voice, and sings.

L I L A C S

Have you seen a purple cloud against a wash of
   willow green
Where sunset spreads its dyes across the western
   world?
Or sought the shadowed freshness of a woodland
   stream,
And scooped up draughts of coolness with your
   fingers curled?

Have you loved the wind, still crisp with frost,
   against your eager lips,
The spray, but recently released, performing its
   ballet?
Or clasped a fragile wine glass, and twirled its
   slender stem,
Inhaling the bewitching fumes, its redolent bouquet?

Then stir yourself to spring-song, and tread the
   lilac lane,
Where lavish earth distills them all, assisted by the
   rain.

L A R G E S S

When dusk draws up its covers from the hollows
    to the hills,
Until the golden head of day is canopied in night,
And firmaments of stars bloom like early daffodils
Above a world of frosty white;

When trees reach out their shadows in a dark caress
Across the undulating curves of naked knoll and
    glade,
To gather in a close embrace their dreaming loveliness,
While the new moon lifts an eyebrow, undismayed;

Though apathetic I step out, indifferent where I go,
As this largess of beauty falls shimmering on the land,
Hope burgeons in my breast, as bright as starlight
    on the snow;
So come, my love, and take my hand!

S U C C E S S I O N

The guttering candles of the night appear
To flicker, as the pre-dawn minutes flow,
And shadow-bearers gather, and bend low
To raise their burden, *Night*, upon his bier.

Weep not his dying, for the past must go
To make way for the future. Hush, to hear
The birds from leafy dimness softly sing
"The king is dead;" louder, *"Long live the king!"*

ANTICIPATION

Speak of the morn,
Now, as the evening closes
Doors to the sun, and sights its rays adorn;
Now, as the dusky cap of evening shrouds us
In fearfulness and faithlessness, reborn,
Speak of the morn!

Speak of the day
Now in the wings, awaiting
Its cue to take the stage and join the play;
Though night conceals the scene of jest and laughter,
And darkly droops its curtain downward, pray
Speak of the day!

DECEPTION

Here are the laces of night-spinning spiders,
Jewelled with droplets of dew or of rain,
Hung from the stems of the half-opened roses—
Yet here lurks pain.

Here twitter birds at the first faintest dawning,
Answering breezes that whisper and sigh,
Turning the leaves to a new morning's chapter
When some must die.

Nothing is ever as safe as its seeming;
Dangers appear in an innocent guise.
Walk ever wary on beguiling pathways—
A word to the wise!

TOTAL ECLIPSE

The world awakens to an azure sky,
To nectar-seeking bees, and insect throngs
Invading pastel-blossomed orchard trees,
To waking birds, testing their skill in songs.

But lo, a shadow creeps across the sun,
And one by one
Birds twitter and fall still.
Retreating to the trees,
They curl their tiny toes,
And under folded wings seek brief repose.
Blooms cradle quiet bees;
Fringed gentians close their sapphire eyes.
Slowly, across the darkening skies,
The brightest stars appear;
Planets shine clear
Where there are no storm clouds to interfere.
Darkness intensifies.
A coolness comes upon the breeze.
The sun, a scimitar of shrinking light
Retires from sight.

In times of old, a feeling of unease
Grew to stark terror, as the aborigine
Saw in the skies an omen of catastrophe—
A sign of punishment for tribal sin
Which, with this evidence, they saw begin.

In ancient wars
Fought by our ancestors
It sapped resolve of legions in the field,
Inducing them to yield,
And giving impetus to fortune's swings
That toppled mighty kings.

What does it mean, this spectacle of awe?
The immutability of nature's law.

As light of day departs, rapid dark bands
Ripple, like shadow waves, across the sands.
Our blinded sun displays a diadem
Of active filaments, like darting flames,
Where luminous gas escapes, and every gem
Appears to sparkle on the rim, which frames
A darkening shutter, placed
Over the source of daylight, now effaced.
Borrowing its jewels, the moon is aureoled
With Baily's beads, a circlet forged of gold.

The beauty of a tranquil night prevails
Until the moon serenely sails
Upon its way, and men with breath indrawn,
Forsaking ancient fear,
Behold a sickle sun appear,
Restoring welcome dawn.

Twilight Vintage

Homeward bound gulls, of coming gloaming hinted,
Pacing the heavens in their outward flight,
While still the seal of day appeared imprinted
On glittering waves, and Huron's rugged height.

Before unnumbered lights of darkness glinted
From constant star, and transient meteorite,
High flared a sacrificial fire, rose-tinted,
Tended by Evening, Darkness' acolyte.

Then flowed the purple juice of twilight, vinted
In cloistered vaults by many a neophyte;
Nor was the wine supply to any stinted,
For day succumbed, and slept, and it was night.

IMPERFECT BEAUTY

The melted flakes of winter gather, swirl,
And tumble in a stream-bed long congealed;
Upon its verge, within each ferny curl,
Lie secret scrolls of summer, unrevealed.

Where snowbanks have so recently receded
A dampness lingers in the mossy green,
And there, the threat of sudden frost unheeded,
Pale pink and white arbutus hides, half seen.

Sharp, glossy quills of grass impale brown leaves,
Like arrows through the heart of summer slain,
Yet here and there disturbed, the dark earth heaves
As trilliums resurrect its soul again.

Sky-like the slough, marsh marigolds to star it,
Dappled the adder's tongues as infant deer;
So beautiful the world, no flaw should mar it:
Where are you, lover, that you are not here?

D A Y B R E A K

Awake!
A final chill
Steals past the shadowy sill....
Birds twitter from the nearby brake....
Emerging from the gloom, the stark panes loom.
Awake, and see dawn bloom!

Arise!
Though umbral shade
Still lingers in the glade,
More lofty darkness shrinks and dies
Upon night's funeral pyre, consumed by fire.
Rise to admire!

F L O T I L L A

The evening sky is shadow grey, and pewter;
The waves are slate, with froth upon each crest;
Grey, too, the driftwood, which that greedy looter,
The sea, has torn from ships its storms distressed.
Tossed on the surges, where they seem minuter
Than toys upon the ocean's heaving breast,
Still distant boats seem barks of some freebooter—
A pirate's ships, returning from their quest.

The homing craft, heaped with their sequined
    plunder,
Trailing their flags of gulls that dip and soar,
With stout prows cleaving wrathful waves asunder,
Seem ships pursued by vengeful gods of yore
Who took the heavens with the sound of thunder,
And churned the seas into a mighty roar;
Until, when near, they lose their ancient wonder,
And turn to fishing boats approaching shore.

WINTER EVENING

From where I sit, 'twixt glow of lamp and fire,
I watch the dim-out of another day:
Dark storm-clouds hovering low,
The tangled blur of branches, shadow-grey
Above the shadowed snow.
This is a state so near the heart's desire,
Here, where the firelight casts its constant glow,
While, like the sea's salt spray,
The vagrant snow-gusts shift, and whirl, and blow,
Then lull, and die away;

That it would seem that pain could not prevail
Nor grief sustain its might
Against the conquering Presence in the gale;
But with the tide
Of day, must ebb defeated into night,
Leaving the healing storm spread far and wide
Across the countryside.

AFTER THE STORM

The snow has swirled across the world,
A great white tide,
Leaving bleached and bloated forms,
Unidentified.
Through the storm the evergreens
Like seagulls strove and cried,
Which now stand conquered, foamy wings
Folded at each side.
It seems aspiring life has died,
                    But suddenly
The wind shakes an avalanche
From a hemlock tree,
And muffled thunder whispers
In the soft white sea;
While branches lift like pinions,
Straining to be free.
Ah, freedom! Wistful dream of that
Which cannot be!

A NORTHERNER SPEAKS

How can you live in the south, and never know
The challenge of the snow?
The drifts piled in the plum like winter bloom;
Night's early gloom;
The rent ice grumbling as the red gauge falls,
And frost at midnight crackling in the walls?

We love this starkness, being surfeited
With violence of yellow, orange, and red.

How can you live in the south, and never know
A crocus framed in snow?
The white of ice-floes on a cobalt sea;
Sap running free?
A migrant finch upon a ragged vine;
Stalactite eaves, dripping where sunbeams shine?

We could not know such joy, did we not long
Through bitter months for color and for song.

S U N - D O G S

The red dogs run on the scent of the sun,
Across a frosty dawn, behind the trees' white lace;
My runners whine down the steep incline,
As I ride into the morning, at my mare's brisk pace.

Snow clods break and scatter in her wake,
Thrown from her hoofs as they rhythmically sway,
While like waves of the sea, to right and left of me,
The snowbanks dip and swell and fall away.

Here and there a fence, spruce and hemlock dense,
Etch violet shadows on the vast, clean white;
And down below, clear-stencilled in the snow,
Go footprints of wild things which hunted in the night.

Looking back, I see our glossy track
Unwinding in a long white scroll;
And all around, like mica on the ground,
A wealth of frost jewels twinkle from each knoll.

My hands grow numb, my lips turn dumb,
Frost rims my hood where my breath congeals,
But each new surprise brings sparkle to my eyes,
In the fairyland of winter which the dawn reveals.

Sinking Of The Dorchester

Feb. 3, 1943

The wind was cold. The Dorchester
Heaved through the icy sea.
The month was February
In 1943;

When off the coast of Greenland,
By enemies attacked,
Her pierced hull filled with water—
A deadly cataract.

The order came, *"Abandon ship!"*
But four were ill-prepared:
All lacked flotation jackets—
A fearful danger shared.

Four chaplains, by their sacrifice
On this random group bestowed
Their life vests. Jew and Gentile,
They shared a common code.

Let guns salute their selflessness
On each Memorial Day,
But let our hearts exalt the faith
Which pointed out the way.

There can be no memorial
Where stormy waters toss,
But raise a flag to honor them,
And lower it for loss.

Bugle notes summon to service in war,
But grieve for its terrible cost:
Reveille, spurring to heroic deeds,
Taps for the valorous lost.

---

*Note: The chaplains, Lt. George L. Fox, 42 (Methodist),
1st Lt. Alexander D. Goode, 31 (Jewish), 1st Lt. Clark V.
Poling, 32 (Reformed Church of America), and 1st Lt.
John P. Washington, 34 (Catholic) went down with the
ship.*

NORTHERN LIGHTS

High in the northern sky,
Eerily flashing, pale
Ribbons of ghostly fire
Surge through the dark.
Wave after wave rolls by,
Lighting the heavens, while
Painting the midnight dome
With pastel hues.

Red banners undulate,
Blue takes erratic paths,
High flare the yellow bands
Into the sky;
Bright spectral surges flow,
Erasing stars from view,
Shaming the moon into
Veiling her face.

Faint wraith-like images
Flicker and flutter,
Spin a pirouette
In ethereal ballet;
Pose in an arabesque,
Leap like lithe dancers,
Then leave the stage in a
Gliding glissade.

S   T   O   R   M

Storm,
What life you overpower!
What trees deform;
What burrows inundate
Where mole or woodchuck cower,
Hostage to fate!
What quail devour
Beneath their mother's battered wing;
What havoc do you sow,
What timber overthrow
Where sparrows cling!
What message do you bring
At terror's height
Of ruin in the night
To countless creatures, held in thrall
By pressure's fateful fall!

DISILLUSIONMENT

So this is life!
A wakening from the careless sleep of youth
To gaze into the mystic eyes of pain;
A pure chant offered upward, through whose peace
Fate's mocking laugh beats out a wild refrain:
So this is life!

So this is love!
A yearning toward the sunset, transient;
Some treasured trinket, broken on the floor;
A sadness sister to the one which creeps
Through thoughts of beauty marred forevermore:
So this is love!

D U S K

Here in the frigid north the twilight lingers
And lays long fingers
Of shadow on the snow.
Reluctant to go,
The daylight hovers on the icy hills;
Late sunlight spills
Across the vistas which my windows frame,
Before night comes to claim
Its realm of glacial starkness;

While in the sultry tropics, far away,
Impatient with delay,
There sweeps across the scene a sudden dark-
ness,
Erasing in a twinkling well-known shapes—
An instantaneous drawing of the drapes
Across the brilliant day.

PASSAGE OF TIME

One April day, I roamed a spring-soft field,
And saw the green upthrusting, blade by
blade....
The turf below my footsteps does not yield.
When did the jonquils fade?

I faltered in my work the other day
To watch two robins build against the sky....
This is November, though I thought it May.
When did the fledglings fly?

I held a poppy to my hair, and smiled
To see my glowing image in the glass....
What it shows now can not be reconciled.
When did my girlhood pass?

CONVERSATION WITH A CHILD

The snowdrifts are going.
"Where do they go?"
Up to the sky where the wild winds blow,
Down to the lake where the ice floes shine,
Into the earth where the dark roots twine.

Whiteness is darkening.
"What will it be?"
Brown of the shallows, blue of the sea,
Yellow forsythia, tulips' red,
Green of flag leaves and fiddlehead.

The silence shatters.
"What is that sound?"
Water trickling along the ground,
Dripping icicles, settling snow,
Whir of bright wings that circle low.

Everything's young again.
"You are old!"
Not when the jonquils erupt in gold;
Not while the redbud flame mounts on high.
You are no younger in spring than I!

D E A F N E S S

The shrill of peepers in a roadside bog,
Loon laughter echoing across the bay,
A partridge drumming on a distant log,
A vesper sparrow's song at close of day;
The noisy tumult of a waterfall,
The sibilance of leaves, stirred by the breeze,
The surge of surf against a stout sea wall—
Slowly, with time, they dim to memories.

Yet, with each loss, some hidden gain transpires.
The dismal cataloging of the news
Is dimly understood: volcanoes, fires
Battles and tidal waves. Deaf ears refuse
To hear the shots, the cries, to tremble under
The awesome augury of distant thunder.

QUERY

From the wide unknown Beyond,
Far above the Milky Way,
Where the dark void wraps bright suns,
And tomorrow's secrets stay;
Mother, do you see your babe
Of yesterday?

She, your second-born, who once
Pliant in her cradle lay;
Future promise in the hope
Baby hands and eyes convey.
Mother, do you mourn her loss
To yesterday?

Searching down the astral aisles
Does your anxious gaze survey
Records of the wasted years,
Idle hands and feet of clay?
Mother, has the vision fled
From yesterday?

From far space where stars are born
Do you witness with dismay
Wayward steps now slow, unsure,
Burnished locks now lichen grey?
Mother, weep, Oh, weep that babe
Lost yesterday.

H E A R T

Heart that fueled my flying feet at the age of four,
Drove my legs to nimbly scale the peaks,
Labored with unfailing strength as you powered
    every chore,
Bore the bloom of youth to brow and cheeks;

Heart which thudded at the glance of admiring eyes,
Quickened in response to each caress,
Melted at each promise sensual need could improvise,
Softened at each sign of tenderness;

Heart which bled at every sign of iniquity,
Yet was always full to bleed once more,
Palpitating to the theme of each new catastrophe,
Aching at the pain the victims bore;

Heart, we long have been a team with a common goal,
Facing daily hazards eagerly;
Always avid for the fray, undertaken, heart and soul:
Traitor! Why have you abandoned me?

JOURNEYS

I took a lonely journey, long forgotten,
Down a canal constricted through its course,
Unwilling to relinquish warm enfoldment,
But urged along by an impelling force.

Now, though lethargic age would bid me linger
Within life's snug embrace, compellingly
A harbinger calls me to leave, and go where
Another lonely journey waits for me.

A C C E L E R A N D O

Gently a snow star slips,
Hesitant, shy,
Tender as love's young lips
To kiss the eye.
Slowly a curtain dips
Over the sky
As the first soft flakes fly.

At the storm's height
Sharp are the darts of the foe—
Needles of white
Piercing the cheeks to a glow.
Sudden as tears in the night
Stingingly flow,
Salt sift the grains of the snow.

M E M O R Y

A glance of tenderness glows evermore
Across the dimming world of memory;
As petals in the dust upon the floor,
Bruised and discolored, do but speak to me
Of scent and honey, summer's fragrant store,
Held ever captive; though the heart must see
With inner vision what the eyes deplore
As lost forever to eternity.